Grief
Speaks...

PASTOR CHRISSY KIDD

Grief Speaks...

Understanding the
language of the broken

XULON PRESS

Xulon Press
555 Winderley Pl, Suite 225
Maitland, FL 32751
407.339.4217
www.xulonpress.com

Paperback ISBN-13: 978-1-66289-298-1
Ebook ISBN-13: 978-1-66289-299-8

To my children- To say I am proud of you would be an understatement. To say I would be lost in this journey without the both of you would be truth. Love you forever- Mom and Dad.

Introduction

GRIEF HAS ITS own language. I came to this realization within days of my husband's accident. When you are grieving, you are desperate to find someone, anyone who can speak the language back to you. Someone who can see the hurt in your eyes and know the depths of the darkness you are feeling. So often, though, there is no one who can speak to the pain and hurt that is crippling your heart and pulsating through your veins. So, you isolate, you shut down, and do not allow the language (i.e., the pain) to flow out, which only makes you feel worse. You convince yourself that keeping it to yourself and swallowing it down would be far better than speaking it out and having someone, unintentionally, inflict more pain on your heart.

Perhaps, it is better to find someone who can understand the language and speak back to your pain. Someone who has witnessed horror and tragedy and will not shrink away. I understand how difficult it is to find people who even have a clue and can listen. I will try my best, friend, in this book to be open and honest with the horror that my eyes have seen. I will caution that this book may not be for everyone, and that is okay. I will also give a warning that if you have experienced trauma and tragedy and if your heart is just not ready yet to read the graphic experience of me and my family, then I understand that, too, and this book may not be for you until you are ready.

Early in my journey through grief, I can remember being in the library with my children. I thought to myself, *I bet there is a book that I can read that might speak to the pain and help me release at least some of it.* I found nothing. It was then that I really determined that a book that specifically talks about the pain of grief and the horror of tragedy was necessary.

I was talking with someone a while ago and she indicated that someone she knew just recently went through a miscarriage. I, too, have miscarried, but rarely ever speak about it. This person asked me a thought-provoking question, "Why do we often not speak about the things that pain us? That mark us?" I found myself telling her that it's because it seems like in life, we often become a part of certain camps.

We all have probably been a part of many camps (e.g., the single camp, the married camp, the college camp, the family camp, etc.), but certain camps, especially the ones involving pain, we tend to keep to ourselves. In my opinion, we stay silent about certain camps that we have been in until it becomes necessary to bring them into the light. For example, I do not talk about my miscarriage until I am trying to bring comfort to someone who has felt the immense pain of losing a baby. Some camps are just too painful for us to talk about unless we have a need to speak.

My goal is to speak about grief. It is a hard language to speak and might possibly bring me more pain, but my hope, my prayer is that through speaking, it will bring comfort, light, and hope to someone who has found themselves in the trenches of grief. Take heart, friend, I know your pain. I hope in some way, while I cannot physically sit with you and hold your hand and let you know how much I understand your despair, that while reading this book you can feel light, love, and peace, and possibly even a good hug which is exactly what you might be desiring right now.

CHAPTER 1

One Beautiful Day

"Why, Lord, do you stand far off? Why do
you hide yourself in times of trouble?"
Psalm 10:1 (NIV)

NOVEMBER 10, 2021 was an absolutely beautiful day in Rushville, Ohio. The sunrise was beautiful and it was unseasonably warm as the sun seemed to just pour down its rays. Everything was alive–the birds, the bugs, the trees. It was an all-around perfect autumn day. To this day, there are days that are similar, and my heart will feel the pain of that day. The same is true for my kids. How can beautiful weather bring deep sadness, you ask? It can when your world shatters on a beautiful day.

That morning, my husband was in his normal playful sorts, especially since we had argued the night before and had not really resolved the issue yet. He was quick to make me want to laugh and move on. I was determined not to let him wear me down and, therefore, not resolve the situation. I know my pride is normal, but I will probably forever regret my attitude that day. He had me cut his hair before going out to work in the shop. I took my time and did the best I could (I am in no way, shape, or form a barber) and I can remember marveling at how handsome he was. As long as I could remember, Jeremy always had a thick head of hair and usually a face full, as well. He was one of very few in our high school years who could even grow a beard, let alone the full one that he always seemed to carry.

He took a shower, got dressed, and headed out to the shop for the day. He had a very large excavator bucket that he was working on and was overjoyed to finally have his concrete shop to properly work in. He had dreamt of the day when he could have his own shop. For years, he had run the business out of his truck as a mobile welder/fabricator. For years, he had suffered through bad weather, mud, and less than ideal on-site conditions as well as a leaky garage and uneven floors if he worked from home. Finally, having the big shop set up and brand-new concrete to work on was like a dream come true. We had worked and prayed for years for this luxury. The big shop was only a month, perhaps two months old.

I, too, got ready for the day and the kids started on their schoolwork. I can remember that while I was still really discouraged from the argument the night before, I had an incredible sense of hope that I had not had for a long time. It had been a really long, rough season for us. I began to work on an issue that we had between our bank and our accounting software that we used for the business. I was frustrated, but, again, kept feeling this overwhelming sense of peace and just a great feeling of something good coming. I can honestly say it felt supernatural.

Before long, Jeremy came in and offered for us to go out to lunch, again, trying to find ways to whittle me down. I declined since it was my prayer and fasting day, and he did not push because he respected and knew how important those days were to me. He informed me that someone was coming soon who was going to look at doing a small job on the big truck. He asked me if I would come out to the shop with him for a bit and I told him, a little frustrated, that I would try and come out soon, but was trying to resolve the issue with the accounting software and the bank. He feigned agitation that I was putting him off, like he always would, and I half chuckled as he walked out. That was the last interaction that I would ever have with my husband. For the record, I would do anything to have that lunch date back.

There is no sugarcoating the fact that seeing your husband's brain matter on the ground has a way of changing you. Sorry, but not sorry if that is too graphic. I do not intend to make light of the tragedy of the day of my husband's accident. I want to be as raw and real as I can possibly be. My reason is because there will be some of you who will read this book, whose eyes have also seen indescribable horror that you can never unsee, and very few people know or understand the terror of this feeling. I, too, know this feeling, friend. I know how sometimes those images wreck your mind and tear through your heart at unexpected moments. I know how it makes your fight or flight response want to kick in. I know how it wrenches your stomach and makes you want to throw up.

If, on the other hand, the story of my husband's accident offends you, then I hope you will search your heart on why it bothers you so much. If it is because real life makes you uncomfortable, then I ask that you lean in and hang on because there is purpose to pouring out the graphic details of that horrid day. Sometimes, we need to lay our thoughts and feelings aside so that we can feel and understand, or at least try to understand, the pain and horror of someone else's experience.

There was so much blood on him that there are blood spatter marks still stained into his work boots even today. I still have moments where my brain tries to wrestle with how this was even possible. When I found Jeremy that day, at the door to the shop, there was nothing that could have ever prepared me for what I would behold. Even now, to bring it back out and relive it, is almost like cutting a knife into my heart. He had somehow made it to the shop door, do not ask me how because he was barely hanging on for life at that point. He looked like something out of a horror movie. His shirt and pants were soaked in blood. His toboggan hat was trying to hold his skull together. All he could do was moan, and where his hand was hanging onto the door handle he had left a horrible bloody handprint.

It is truly a wonder that I did not go into shock right there, just seeing him in that state. It was so graphic that it felt unreal. Like some horrible, terrible dream. I turned around, yelling for the kids, and ran to the house to get my phone. When I got to the door of the house, I burst in and yelled to the kids to come quick because something awful had happened to their dad. I grabbed my phone off of the counter and fumbled to dial 911 as I raced back down to the shop. From that moment on, it was kind of like I was in a tunnel. Like my brain knew I was there, but at the same time was trying to disassociate from the situation. I learned later this is a coping mechanism. It is a natural way for your body to try and protect you from the trauma.

I began the process of trying to piece together what on earth had happened so I could inform the 911 operator and the emergency crew that was headed our way. My daughter was frantically trying to get ahold of family to alert them and my sweet, precious son dropped to his knees and began crying out to God for his daddy. It seemed like an eternity for the squad and the police to arrive, but it was probably only a matter of minutes. They tried to get Jeremy to walk to the ambulance, but when they realized that he could not, they pulled out the stretcher.

The police deduced that he had been cutting apart metal on a very large equipment bucket that he was preparing to fix, and a freak thing happened. The metal had broken loose with such force that Jeremy took a fatal blow to the head. There was evidence that the force had actually thrown him some distance across the shop. The surgeon at the hospital claimed that he never saw what hit him and that he was already pretty much gone when I found him. This should maybe bring me some degree of comfort, but they did not see what I saw that day. I saw the love of my life, fumbling around and moaning with panic in his eyes because even if he was not coherent, his body knew something horrible had happened. The death certificate later would tell me that he died instantaneously. Again, the coroner never witnessed the horror that my eyes and the eyes of my children will never unsee as we watched him flail around panicked and us completely helpless on how to help him.

I swear it was like he knew. He knew something terrible had happened and there was no turning back. They got him into the squad on the stretcher and began administering life-saving measures. I saw his brain matter on the plate outside where he had been welding and turned around to vomit outside the big shop door. One of the emergency workers came over and asked me a question I will never forget, "Can't stand the sight of blood, huh?" I believe that was the exact moment that anger became a part of me. I cooly responded that I thought it was a little more than the sight of blood, at which, to my complete surprise, he indicated that he had seen way worse. Maybe he was trying to keep me from going into shock, that is my hope at least.

Everything after that seemed like a blur. As they proceeded working on Jeremy in the squad, I began trying to contact people and console my children. Thankfully, we had support that showed up and did the best they could to try to help us in such a terrible situation. It was determined that if Jeremy was to have any chance of survival, then he would have to be life flighted. Then began the arduous wait for the helicopter. Thankfully, there was an open grass field on our property that had plenty of room to land the helicopter. They had to sedate Jeremy because he kept fighting them in the squad while they were trying to save his life. I remember vividly holding my son when they opened the doors to the squad to get Jeremy loaded onto the helicopter and trying to assure him in all of the ways that I could, but I think in his heart, he knew.

I barely saw Jeremy when they loaded him onto the helicopter. I was scared to death, but honestly, did not believe that he would never come back home. I mean, we had had scares before in our married life. None quite to this level, but God always showed up. Always. It could be the eleventh hour, when all hope was just about lost, but God always came through. I think, honestly, I still had this thought in my brain, even though my gut was telling me otherwise. I kept thinking that this was probably going to be an almost impossible road, but God had always been faithful and He would get us through. Foolishly, we think we have such a firm foundation in our faith, such a firm grasp on God and life until those foundations get obliterated by a life circumstance. A nightmare that suddenly is not a dream where you are going to wake up and be relieved it was just a dream. No, a real-life horror that becomes reality for you and your children.

I have sobbed while writing this portion. To open back up the layers of pain and the horror of that day is a bitter pill. Why do it? Let me tell you, for my healing and for yours. Sometimes, we need to be real about the horrors that we experience in our lives to bring peace and healing to someone else. I am hopeful that by being honest about my pain, and the tragedy my family experienced and now face daily, I will bring some kind of comfort and healing to whatever awful life circumstance you might be currently facing. And if you are fortunate enough not to have had to deal with something like this before, then ask God to let this teach you empathy for those who do face these horrible situations.

I have been ghosted by people. I have been avoided in a store or public place. I have gotten used to just not acknowledging anyone in public anymore unless they seek me out. I know it is because we often do not know what to say. I get that, and I have been guilty of doing the same. I also know that sometimes someone else's tragedy brings us face to face with our own mortality and the realization of the frailty of life. But what we fail to realize is that the road of the widow who has lost a spouse and the road of a child who has lost a parent is such a lonely road, especially when our new status makes others very uncomfortable. Please remember, as a human being and especially as a Christian, someone else's pain is not about you. This is about you being like Jesus, or at least a kind human being, and having compassion for others. One thing is for certain, Jesus is not afraid nor does He not know what to say to a widow and a child. Church, we have got to do better. Humans, we have got to do better.

We love the story in the Bible about Shadrach, Meshach, and Abednego, right? Where they stand up to the king, he throws them in the fiery furnace, God shows up and protects them, and they come out of the furnace not even smelling like smoke? If you have never read this story, you can find it in chapter 3 of the book of Daniel. But, friends, here is a truth you need to know. Sometimes, you will go through the fire, you will come out smelling like smoke, and your smoke smell might be offensive to others.

I have had people promise to do things and never show up. Friends, you need to know if you promise a widow that you are going to do something, she does not have a plan B. You are it. And I understand because, sadly, I have done the same thing before I knew the awful truth of how hard and lonely this road really is. Scripture even commands us to care for the widow and the fatherless/motherless, right (Jas. 1:27)? Usually, we think that means money, but the truth is, often, money is not what they need. They need love, grace, understanding, mercy—absolutely everything you would hope to receive if the tables were turned. The truth is, life is busy and people are preoccupied. I get that, I do. But life does not stop just because your husband or wife dies and your children lose their father or mother.

If you are a widow, friend, I send you my heart because you, too, know this pain all too well. I know those feelings of abandonment and rejection that you possibly have been feeding yourself in your grief journey. I am just hopeful that by telling the truth, it will help make a change instead of perpetuating the model that somehow widows are just "so strong" and, therefore, able to get through this. Or especially if you are an older widow, people will just expect that perhaps you will not live long after your spouse and that is okay because that is the way life goes. Or is it?

What if we actually flipped the script, were obedient to the things God and humanity has called us to do, and gave to those who are in need? Does it cost? Yes, of course, but is it not worth helping someone walk through the darkness? Is that not what you would hope for if you were walking the same road? Perhaps these are some things to ponder and some questions to seek out in your own soul.

CHAPTER 2

The Family Consult Room

"Hear my prayer, Lord; listen to my cry for mercy. When I
am in distress, I call to you, because you answer me."

Psalms 86:6-7 (NIV)

I AM NOT A screamer. Never have been. Actually, growing
up, I had a certain fear that if there was a moment where I
would have to scream, would I even be able to do so? I have had
dreams, intense dreams, where I am in a terrible situation, and
I am unable to scream, and I wake up frightened.

It took what seemed like years to make it to the hospital.
Because I was not in my right mind, I for some reason led my
dad to take the really long way to Grant Hospital. What do you
talk about when you just witnessed something awful happen
and you are now going to the hospital? How do you even feel?
You try and feel hopeful, yes, but you also feel a very large weight
of apprehension weighing down on you.

I remember Dad and I would be talking, and I would feel
this horrible feeling of dread come over me and I thought I
would vomit. Dad would tell me, "Hold on, babe. It is going to

be okay." Upon arrival, we had to find a place to park. Thankfully, my father-in-law had arrived first and was able to give us some direction on where to go. My brother had also arrived ahead of us. As I stepped out of my dad's truck and made my way to the doors of the hospital, that feeling of dread gripped me and it felt like I had lead weights in my feet and legs. I knew I was moving forward, one step at a time, but it felt like I was standing still.

We entered the hospital and there were nurses standing there waiting for me. Dad and I had to go through security, of course something on him would set off the metal detector, and we would have to spend minutes, that seemed more like hours, trying to get past security. There was a woman standing there waiting on us, too, which later I would find out was the hospital chaplain. For the life of me, I never expected what would happen next.

They led me down a hallway, which felt like one of the longest walks of my life, and as soon as I saw the family consult room, I had this feeling that it was not going to be good. I honestly think I was expecting they would tell me he was in bad shape and had a long road to go, but nothing prepared me for what was about to be said. We walked into the room and my dad sat down in a chair. My father-in-law came into the room and I remember seeing his eyes as he simply said, "He didn't make it, babe."

Wait, what? What does "he didn't make it" mean? It was then the full force of the realization that my husband was gone hit me like a Mack truck and from somewhere inside of me came a scream, maybe more like a wail, that I have never heard come out of me before. My father-in-law embraced me and held me as I screamed and cried into his shoulder. I do not even think there were any tears. There is a sorrow you can experience that is so dark and so deep that your soul cannot even produce tears.

I remember hearing my dad back in the corner weeping, too. The intensity of the moment caused the chaplain to step out. It is a moment etched in my memory forever that I wish was never, ever etched on my brain. In that moment, the humanity of two of the strongest men I have ever known in my life came pouring out of them. I am not even sure "nightmare" is a proper word to describe the moment. I mean, I have had some terrible nightmares in my lifetime, but the thing about a nightmare is you get to wake up and feel the overwhelming relief that it was not reality.

This was my reality; this was their reality. None of us would get to wake up and realize that it was all just a really bad dream. I did not "cry" long, and the chaplain came back in and asked if we would want to see him. I almost said no, that I had already seen enough to last me a lifetime back at the house, but I knew seeing him and praying over him was what I needed to do. I am so thankful I followed my leading. I walked into the room where they had him, which I think was not far at all from the family consult room, and I looked at my big, strong, handsome husband lying there on the bed, lifeless. Lifeless. No smile on his face. No laughter in his eyes, which thankfully were closed. No joke to crack and tell me I worry too much. Just lifeless.

I know the hospital staff did the best they could to clean him up. I know this because my dad would later comment that he could not imagine what the kids and I had seen at the house because to him, Jeremy looked awful. But again, he did not see the horror we had witnessed. They had done their best to clean the blood off and they had tried to bandage his head up the best they could. He still had the tubes up his nostrils and down his throat and his eyes were horribly swollen, but it was his eyes that gave me exactly what I believe God needed me to see.

Jeremy was at peace. I cannot really describe it other than there was a look around his eyes. In recent years, his eyes had come to wear the mark of dark circles due to stress, yet in that moment, the dark circles were not there. He had just suffered an immense amount of trauma, and even though his eyelids were completely black and blue, under his eyes it looked like he finally got good sleep. I knew, knew, knew in my heart at that moment that he chose to go home. I also knew that if our roles had been reversed, I would have chosen to go home as well.

Friend, if your time on this earth ended today, would the thought of eternity bring you peace, or would there be dread? Is the desire of your heart to meet King Jesus, or is He a nonexistent part of your life? These are questions that all of us will need to answer at some moment in our life. The moment when our humanity gets the best of us and our time on this earth expires. I have no other hope to give than Jesus.

My husband, Jeremy, was not a perfect man, but he loved Jesus with all of his heart. When the moment of his passing came, his heart went to the one who loved him best, and I believe he was welcomed with open arms. The peace around his eyes would be a reassurance that my broken heart would need multiple times in my grieving.

I walked up to the bed and tried to hold his hand. At that moment, I was desperate for care. Jeremy was my rock. We met on the bus in the eighth grade, and I had been crazy about him pretty much since. He was always my comfort, always my companion, always quick to make me laugh. He used to say all of the time that hearing me laugh was his favorite thing. I touched his hand and the coldness was like a slap in the face. There was no warmth, no life, and in that moment began the bitter loneliness that is the fruit of grief.

I let go of his hand and placed my hands on the bed-rail instead and prayed over him. To this day, I do not remember the words that the Holy Spirit poured out of my broken heart, but I do remember vividly telling God that His ways are not my ways and His thoughts are not my thoughts, and while I did not understand, I thanked God for Jeremy and released him.

See, God did not need me to release Jeremy to Him, Jeremy was already with God. The release was about me, and so began my struggle to trust in the aftermath of that horrible day. You do not watch your husband get his head bashed in and not question your faith. God had always shown up. Always. So, it makes you ask, "Why not here, God? Where was the miracle this time? Did You abandon us? Have You forsaken us? Do You care? Where are You?!"

These are questions that I have had to hold and continue to hold tension with as I navigate the choppy and uncharted waters of grief. I have heard grief comes in waves and there is some truth to this in my experience, but if you have acutely felt those waves, you would say they often come like a tsunami—eager to take you down and determined to take you out. I have felt that tsunami, friend, in all of its disastrous force, and somehow, someway the waves have not overtaken me. Do not let them overtake you. Even if in your true heart, if you are able to be honest, there are many, many times your desire is to succumb to those bitter waters and let them suffocate the life right out of you.

This is real life. This is raw grief. Not the primped and polished version that, so often, our public side likes to portray. Not the primped and polished version that I showed at my husband's viewing and memorial service. No one really likes to admit the broken, bitter, angry, sobbing, wailing, snot-dripping, screaming, devastated, laying on the floor, wrenching, dry-heaving monster that takes up residence in your very soul when you have experienced this kind of grief. It is not pretty. It does not feel good. It feels like someone is trying to kill you. It feels like even though you are running as fast as you can to save your life, your greatest fear is that it will win and it will kill you.

If you have never felt this kind of grief before, be thankful, and for the love of everything, be patient and empathetic with those who are in the throes of grief. Do not walk away from them because their bitterness makes you uncomfortable. Embrace them. Listen to them. Check in on them. Because if you love them, then this is 100 percent about them and 0 percent about you. Do not take from them. Do not make their already difficult lives even more complex with your issues. This is the epitome of a terrible situation. Do not try to make them feel better (like somehow you could), and above all else, do not try to brighten or make light of the situation. Your loved one needs you to feel their pain and help them to carry the load, in their time and in their way. It really is awful, and there are things in this life that do not just "work out."

CHAPTER 3

The Worst Conversation

"...They will look up to heaven and down at the
earth, but wherever they look, there will be
trouble and anguish and dark despair."
Isaiah 8:21-22 (NLT)

A POEM MY SON, Eli, wrote shortly after the accident:

I would cross the earth if I knew you were on the other side. I
have seen so much my eyes have gotten wide.

Your life is a book, and You, God, are the Author. But life is so
hard without you, Father.

Father, where have you gone? Did you forget me? I tried to
stop time, but you say that you're happy.

As life goes by, I'll never forget about you. When I fell apart,
Dad, you were the glue.

Why did you leave when I was so broken? Now that you're gone, emotion has woken.

Dad, I always bragged of how cool you are. But now that you've left, you seem so far.

I try to learn things on my own. I wish you were here, and I could be shown.

Dad, I really wish you were here. I want your presence and wish you were near.

"Eli, wake up and open your eyes. Everything is well." I hear your voice, Dad, but life without you feels like hell.

Satan, are you proud of killing my father? They say the Lord works miracles, but when everything happened, He did not bother.

Satan, I hope you're happy forever after because we are not. Just thinking of this makes me feel red hot.

I love you, Dad, and I miss every bit of you. You always helped me make decisions, but, Dad, now I don't know what to do.

I love you, Dad.

How on earth do I tell the children? This was the thought that hit me the moment I walked out of the hospital. I had two babies at home (thirteen and sixteen at the time) anxiously waiting for me back at the house. I knew they were hoping that while it was a horrible situation that their dad had survived and he would be coming home. The last thing I had told my son as they were loading my husband into the helicopter was, "Listen to me, Bub. They would not take him if they did not have hope that he will survive." How was I going to go home and tell him that his dad was never coming back? That the horrible memory he had of his dad, stumbling around broken and bloodied at the shop door, would be the last image he would ever have of his father alive?

No chance to say goodbye. No closure. Literally, everything you fear that your children would have to see, actually maybe even more than you fear, is now their reality. You do so much to provide the best for your children. You try to protect them. You try to give them the best, innocent childhood that you possibly can, yet in an instant, terror has stripped them of the security they once knew. Their dad was their best friend, to the both of them. He loved them unconditionally. He taught them so much about the world. Things like how to work hard, provide, love their mom, do what was right, stand up against what was wrong, and how to love and encourage like Jesus. He taught them how to laugh and have a good time even when things were difficult. People prized us for being such a close family, and now our family was splintered with pain.

Once I knew my husband was gone, my children were my number one priority. I was desperate to get home to them, even though I dreaded the news that I would have to somehow deliver. There is no parenting class on what to do in a crisis situation or how to tell your children that their dad or mom died. I also worried that people who had already heard the bitter news about Jeremy's passing would begin to show up at our house before I would make it there to tell them the news. Everything had happened so fast, and it seemed like everyone was still in shock and confused about how anything like this could have happened.

When Dad pulled the truck into the driveway, the kids were out sitting on the swings with my mom. As I stated before it was a beautiful day, the dogs were running and barking, glad to see us, and the kids had a look of complete confusion on their faces about why we were home so soon. My mom's face went from surprise to knowledge as I could tell she knew there was no way we should be coming home. I got out of the truck and, again, that lead-footed feeling was there. I walked over to the swings and watched their sweet, confused faces. The words that came out of my mouth was, "Your dad didn't make it."

Again, the phrase "he didn't make it." I wish I could put into words what that feeling feels like, but until you have felt the horror of that phrase, you cannot really understand the pain of it. Imagine for a moment, if you can, having to let words come out of your mouth that will forever mark and change your children. I will not put into words how they reacted because that is not my story to tell, but I can for sure imagine that it was like telling them that the hopes and dreams of our family were shattered and our lives would never, ever be the same. All of the things Jeremy and I had tried to protect them from, yet we were powerless in protecting them from one of the worst things that they will perhaps ever experience in their life.

Widowed and fatherless became our titles and those titles will ruffle the feathers of those who have never had to accept those titles before. There is a weight to those titles, though, that must be properly processed through, no matter how painful the process. As I have already stated, Scripture talks about the widow and the fatherless, but in real life, those terms make Christians uncomfortable. Still, they are realities in this broken world that the church cannot turn their backs on just because it makes them uncomfortable. Life is hard and bad things happen; this is just reality.

Friend, if you have had something tragic happen to you and your children, please let them grieve. Do not put them on display and get them to try to act a certain way. Let them weep and express their emotions in whatever way they need to. Protect them from well-meaning people in their life who have no clue what is best for them, but will try and lead them through a process they know nothing or very little about.

My little family benefited from us going through the process together, speaking with a therapist and going through family counseling, and me allowing them the freedom to grieve how they needed. We also found comfort in keeping that strong, close connection that their dad had fought so hard to instill in us. It will look different for your family, but please do what is best for them.

CHAPTER 4

The Longest Night

"O God, listen to my cry! Hear my prayer! From the ends of the
earth, I cry to you for help when my heart is overwhelmed."
Psalms 61:1-2a (NLT)

WHERE IS GOD? Where is He in my darkest need? Why
does it seem like He hides when we are in dark distress?
That whole evening after the accident, we had friends come and
go. It is a curious thing watching people try to figure out what
on earth to do because they had no clue how to help in this
situation.

"Do you want food?" No, who could think about eating at a
time like this?

"Do you want to be left alone?" Absolutely not, because then
you have to face the crashing reality.

How do you help someone when they are living a nightmare?

I would try to talk or even joke (my normal coping mechanism for highly stressful situations), but then that gut-wrenching
reality check would hit me in the stomach and I would grow
quiet. If I even put food to my mouth, I felt like throwing up. I

felt like someone had grabbed ahold of my insides and mangled them and my body was somehow, someway just trying to survive. My brain felt like a permanent fog had permeated every possible space in my head and to even make a simple decision was exhausting. I knew at some point, though, that everyone would go home and the kids and I would be left to face this darkness alone.

After everyone had left, I laid on my bedroom floor, wrapped in my husband's coat, and waited for the kids to get ready for bed. If I am honest, at that moment, I wanted to die. I tried to cry, yet it was like my body was wracked with grief but all out of tears. I knew all three of us were dreading the thought of going to bed, me especially, crawling into our bed alone. I suggested to the kids that perhaps we should sleep together. Thankfully, they agreed and for the first time since they were little, I had my children in bed with me.

That first night was wretched. I would just get done consoling the one, they would be exhausted, and would go to sleep, then the other would wake up sobbing. I lay there in the middle going back and forth; meanwhile, I was so angry at God that I could have spit at Him. I tried to pray and… silence. I tried to feel His presence… I felt nothing. Again, this part may make some of you uncomfortable, but I want to be raw and real for every single person who has had to face this kind of tragedy and knows exactly the feelings that I am sharing.

Again, I repeat, we foolishly think we are so strong in our faith, until the foundations of our faith, at least what we have believed to be true, are obliterated and we are left feeling like we have been abandoned and lied to. I was seething angry, yet shattered and broken all at the same time. Where was our miracle? We had done everything we were told to do. We were faithful with every part of our lives, we played the game by the rules, so why were we forsaken? It was the longest night of my life, and I had no revelation, vision, comfort, or anything. Just what felt like darkness and silence.

At some point I must have finally drifted off to sleep for a time and woke up to my son watching videos of his dad on his dad's phone. Thankfully, my husband loved to laugh and make others laugh, so his phone was full of videos of himself. The three of us sat there and watched them. We laughed some, then just sobbed and cried. It was the first time that I really thought that I was not going to survive my husband's passing. Grief will make you feel like dying; that is the truth.

Grief will make you feel angry. It will do things to your body and your brain that make you feel like you are going crazy. You have moments when you feel like you are dying, then you have moments when you actually want to die. You will feel sick. You may have zero desire to eat. You will feel exhausted almost all of the time. You will try to sleep, but sleep will evade you. You will want people around, then you will resent their presence. You will cry out to God, then be angry at His seeming disregard. It is so hard!

The partially healed part of me wants to speak up at this point, but for this book, I am going to refrain because so many books on grief will skirt by or merely brush the pain that is felt in grief and then be eager to move forward with the healing. I am learning the language of the healed, but for this book, my goal is the language of grief because I want you to know, friend, I feel your hurt! I have felt your pain and the horror of it all! Part of the healing is being seen and acknowledged—to have people who are not afraid of the terror that you have had to face and be a safe space for you to puke all of that out.

If you are reading this part and your pain is bursting at your insides, I want you to know that it is okay to feel that way! It is okay to say this is horrible and hurts like hell and I am angry! I know what it feels like to scream and throw things and shake my fist at God! I know what it feels like to be completely surrounded by others who have absolutely no idea what you are going through, yet they want to "fix" something that they have no power to "fix"! I, instead, want to tell you that I understand and, friend, I will not try and "fix" you because the truth is, you are not broken. I know you feel broken right now. I know you might feel like you have been shattered into a thousand pieces and there is no hope for you. But I can tell you that there is hope. You are going to make it because you, my friend, are stronger than you think.

We say all of the time that there is beauty that comes from ashes. But what I have learned is there is beauty in the ashes, but you have to be brave enough to look. God is good, and my circumstances and your circumstances do not determine His goodness. He is just good and His love and favor for you continues.

This road is hard, but not even Jesus was spared the realities of the cruelness of this life. It does not mean that you should give up because life is worth living. Healing will come when you are ready. Give yourself grace and hold on to Jesus, even if it is only the hem of His robe!

CHAPTER 5

See the Hurt

"O God my rock," I cry, "why have you forgotten me? Why
must I wander around in grief, oppressed by my enemies?"
Psalm 42:9 (NLT)

W E HAVE THIS sentimental saying that you need to be
kind because you have no idea what someone may be
going through. Do we really believe that, though? Do we think
that we can look into someone's eyes and see their hurt? See
their pain? I believe we can, but often we choose not to because
it makes us feel uncomfortable. We often say things like, "I don't
want to say anything because I don't want them to feel worse."
False. You do not say anything because of how it makes you feel.

I have been thankful on this journey for people who can
see, or even sense, my pain. I have had a couple of times when
someone has felt strongly for me because of the leading of the
Holy Spirit. And if we are honest, when you are in true pain, you
cannot cover it up. There is no amount of expensive make-up
that can cover up those dark circles under your eyes (believe me,
I've tried).

It was only two days after the accident, and I had to get us out of our house. My son had already gone with my parents, and my daughter and I were heading out a short time later. We were going to spend the weekend at their house. My daughter and I made a quick trip to the grocery store merely to grab a coffee before we hit the road. I was desperate to get us out of town, but was also sensitive to her coffee needs. In grief, you find yourself trying to find some kind of joy, some kind of semblance of normal. These "joys" often come in little things like simply getting your favorite coffee.

I was so paranoid we would run into someone we knew that I was a mix between an almost deer-in-the-headlights panic and an overwhelmed brain-dead zombie. Sure enough, we were waiting for our coffee and a sweet couple we knew came through the doors of the store. I tried to play cool, perhaps they would not see me. I quickly realized, no, they very much knew we were there. And from the corner of my eye, I watched this exchange of sorts between the two of them.

At first, I think they were dealing with the shock of seeing us. It was just two short days after the accident, and here we were standing in a store waiting for coffee. I could see the heartbreak on their faces for us and could imagine they struggled for a minute to try to gain their composure. We always tend to think we have to be strong for the other person in order to be effective; however, this is completely not true. I knew they were uncertain of what to do. Speaking to us and somehow causing more harm would be incomprehensible, but to go on and not say anything would be like committing a crime.

I do not really remember who made the first move, the couple or us, but at that moment, they were exactly what we needed. As I have stated before, people say grief comes like waves, and yes, I agree there is some truth to this, but in the beginning of grief, it is more like a constant drowning. We embraced the couple, showed the hurt in our eyes, and taking an honest moment to feel the horror with two people who loved us so deeply was a little healing balm for our souls.

I could feel my anxiety subside slightly in their genuine care for us. Are we even looking for pain in the eyes of the people we encounter every day? Pain and grief are uncomfortable, yes, absolutely. But I need you to remember that one day, it is going to knock on your door, or perhaps already has, and you are going to wish that someone could look past the make-up and fake smile and see right into your pain.

People who are grieving need to be seen. They need to have the deep well of pain in their soul validated, not chastised away or willingly unnoticed. We talk about people being "stuck in their grief," but maybe it is not that they are stuck. Maybe it is that no one has taken the time and energy to just let them process through the grief openly in whatever way is beneficial to them.

Again, try and remember that one day, you may be walking in the same shoes, and how you treat others should be a direct representation of how you would want to be treated if you were in the same or similar situation. Please give grace, love, and mercy to those who are grieving in your life. They might be relatives, friends, co-workers, or even people who serve you in your community. Empathy should always be the code of the day, especially those of us who claim the title of "Christian."

In scripture, Jesus showed empathy every single time someone was grieving. He gave care, provided for needs, and even wept with those who were weeping. He did not shy away from grief. He did not shy away from hard and uncomfortable situations. No, instead, He knew those were the people who needed His tender care and He acted accordingly. That is why Jesus instructed in His sermon on the Mount, "God blesses those who mourn, for they will be comforted" (Matthew 5:4 NLT). I pray we learn to be the same.

CHAPTER 6

The Sleepless Nights

"But those who trust in the Lord will find new strength.
They will soar high on wings like eagles. They will run
and not grow weary. They will walk and not faint."
Isaiah 40:31 (NLT)

A JOURNAL ENTRY FROM about eight months out:

"'You are going to get through this...' should be
a statement of encouragement, right? Um, to
someone who is grieving, perhaps not so much.
Of course, you know you will get through this, or
at least you hope (and then sometimes you do
not hope). I mean, you almost never hear about
someone dying from a broken heart, right? Unless
you want to track how many elderly couples pass
soon after the death of their spouse. The grief
often seems bad enough that you just might die
(or perhaps even feel like you want to die). Or
perhaps the lack of sleep will take you out. Or

the heart palpitations from the anxiety or stress. Or the lack of eating because you have no desire to eat or even the energy to make yourself something to eat. You want to just sleep, yet even that often gets denied from you. When you are used to sharing your bed and suddenly your bed is empty. You get used to even the sound of their breathing. You take for granted rolling over to your spouse when you've had a bad dream to be comforted. You long to be cuddled and comforted by the very one you are dying now without. 'You are going to get through this...' What if I don't want to?"

One thing I wished someone, anyone really, would have told me is that when you are grieving, a common issue is you do not sleep well. I mean, it makes sense; when you lose your spouse, you no longer have the person sleeping next to you that has possibly been for years. Sharing the covers, sharing the space, listening to them breathe... and then silence. It feels like you could drown in the silence, except your mind will not let you be at peace. You fight your best fight, but no matter how tired you feel, it is like your body just cannot rest. I have never in my life had sleeping issues. I have always been one that as soon as my head would hit the pillow, I would go almost right to sleep. My husband used to envy that about me. Grief stole that from me for months.

Then when I finally overcame my issue of going to sleep, like clockwork, something would wake me up between 3:00-4:00 a.m. repeatedly. That is when, what I will call, the hijacks would come. I call them hijacks because that is exactly what it felt like, as if someone was trying to attack or rob me. I would wake up and, before I could stop myself, would relive the trauma of the accident. It was awful. It also is, unfortunately, normal. Your subconscious can sometimes act like an enemy.

Trauma is a tricky word in our society. Trauma tends to refer to things like abuse in childhood, and I in no way want to belittle or take away from that. But I do not have another good word to describe what it was like emotionally, mentally, or spiritually witnessing the aftermath of my husband's accident. Oh, so many nights I would startle awake, and he would be there in my mind: beaten, bloody, and unable to communicate to me what was wrong. It was like having the accident on repeat in my mind, and I would just roll over and sob in my pillow.

In those moments, if I am raw and honest, I wanted to die. People have called me strong, but in those moments, I clung to God and pleaded with Him that I could not handle the despair. I prayed for the episodes to leave me. I prayed that God would grant me peace, but looking back, I realize that He could not necessarily grant my request. Instead, I believe He was there with me in those bitter moments and His heart was breaking for my agony. We know this feeling, on a much smaller scale, as parents when our children are experiencing something that we desperately want to fix, but we cannot.

Finally, it got so bad and I had tried so many things that I brought it up to the counselor. He, in turn, indicated it was probably time to see a doctor. I never went on medication, though, because once I opened up to the counselor about the struggle, it was like it released me and I no longer dealt with the issue. Often in our life when we speak out about something, it brings peace and release. So often we keep things hidden and to ourselves, mostly because we have shared about other things, and we have been hurt by the reaction, or non-reaction, of others.

But a part of processing grief is getting things out, speaking about the deep pain in your heart, voicing your fears, and hopefully finding empathy from another human being. You must face the pain, and, friend, I know how horribly awful that can be. Please, by all means, get help through a counselor, doctor, minister, grief group, and/or medication. If you have been struggling to get help, I release you from any shame you might be feeling. Grief is excruciatingly hard, and we were never meant to carry that burden alone. Do not be afraid to get the help you need because getting help shows true strength, rather than trying to handle everything on your own. Please take care of you because no one else can do it for you.

CHAPTER 7

The Long Months Ahead

"Turn to me and have mercy, for I am alone and in deep distress."
Psalm 25:16 (NLT)

FROM A JOURNAL entry about five months after the accident...

> "The kids just sent me a video of Jeremy carrying
> me up the steps. I am laughing so hard. He looks
> so real like I could reach out and touch him. I am
> *so lonely.* I have not slept well this week and I
> almost fear going to sleep. I feel like I am going
> crazy with no one here to put me back on track.
> Jeremy usually helped me process through my
> craziness. I feel like a beautiful tree that has had
> a sharp axe taken to its trunk and it has been sev-
> ered abruptly. The top part is laying there, with-
> ering, and dying a slow painful death. It cannot
> be connected back to the base. It is hopeless for
> its survival. The base is also dying because it is

now separated from the rest of the tree. That was
its purpose! It cannot have another purpose, and
now, all of it is wasted! The top, the bottom, the
tragedy of the axe, all just wasted and hopeless!
It does not matter how deep the roots have gone,
there is no saving the tree! God, where are You?!
Help me! I cannot do this!"

"Time of death: Within seconds to minutes of the accident."
I looked at those words again on the death certificate and the
pain was immediately there. Seven months later, and those
simple words still had enough power to make me want to silently
sob in my basement for the next however long. See, here is the
thing about someone's death, life does not stop just because their
life stopped. Bills still need to be paid. Children still need care.
Business details still need to be attended to. Countless decisions
need to be made. Now, those decisions must be made without
your spouse, and that feels debilitating.

I was finally to the point where I needed to swap the titles of
some of the vehicles from my husband's name to mine and I had
to put my eyes on that dreaded death certificate again. Logically,
I would have liked a few moments with the coroner to explain
that if Jeremy had died within "seconds to minutes" of his accident, then someone needed to explain to me what my children
and I saw when we found him at the door of the shop. Blood
everywhere, his head split open, his eye bulging and swollen shut,

and him moaning like he was trying to tell me something, but could not get the words out.

On the one hand, perhaps I should be thankful that he did not feel the way he looked, according to the surgeon and the coroner, at least. According to a secondhand story I had heard from the surgeon, "Jeremy didn't know what had hit him." I do not know because I never got to talk with the surgeon. Yes, it brought me a certain degree of peace thinking about Jeremy not feeling or knowing, but not enough peace for me or my children considering the horror of what we had to witness that day.

We are people who want to know things like, why? Why did we have to witness him in that state? Would it have been better for us to have found him already gone? Would it have been easier for us not to have endured the agony of finding him? The agony of the 911 call? The agony of waiting for the squad? The agony of waiting for the life flight? On that one day alone, it feels like my children and I endured enough agony for a lifetime.

But somewhere in this nightmare, someone said something that resonates now. They said that the fact that Jeremy held on so long was a testament of his love for us and that he did not want to leave us. It was not until they gave him a sedative, so they could calm him enough to be able to start caring for his injuries because, of course, he was fighting them, that he relaxed enough to let us go. He was always fighting for us. I honestly believe to him, that was his number one job and he took it seriously. And now, I am the fighter and feeling so unequipped for the job. Regardless, I mustered up the courage to take that death certificate to the BMV to get the titles transferred from his name to mine. Just another day in the life of a single parent and a grieving widow.

CHAPTER 8

The Firsts Feel Like Forever

"How beautiful on the mountains are the feet of the
messenger who brings good news, the good news of peace
and salvation, the news that the God of Israel reigns!"
Isaiah 52:7 (NLT)

T HE FIRSTS ARE the worst. My husband died in early
November, right before the beloved holiday season. Also
my absolute favorite time of the year. I had someone tell me that
it was such a terrible time to lose someone, and I can remember
blurting out that anytime of the year is a terrible time to lose a
loved one. Thanksgiving came just weeks after the accident, and
I found myself wishing that we could just skip the whole holiday
season. Thanksgiving Day found me tired, extremely sad, and
numb from the ocean of tears I had been crying. I felt like I was
having an out-of-body experience, like my body was there, but
Chrissy was not.

Grief brings such a fog that you become frustrated at the lack
of seeming to be able to have a conscious thought. You forget
the simplest of things, then become frustrated with yourself.

You want to sleep and sleep, yet seem to find no rest, and you become frustrated with yourself. You have days when you set out to accomplish great things, then you tire quickly, and, yep, you guessed it, you become frustrated with yourself. Usually, we are good and quick at offering grace to others, yet have such a hard time extending that hand of grace to ourselves. People around us often do not understand, and sometimes worse, they become frustrated with us.

The firsts cut two ways. First, they cut because you are acutely aware of how everything has changed due to your loss, and they will never be the same. Two, they cut because you are already exhausted with the day to day, let alone having to somehow muster up the strength to survive the firsts. You will find that even on holidays or special occasions that were not important in the past will suddenly become a day of struggle because you are still acutely aware that the day is not the same.

Special days can be extremely difficult. I can remember my first birthday after my husband had passed. His birthday was only two days after mine, and I can vividly remember not wanting to celebrate that birthday. The Lord spoke to me, though, and said, "So, we cannot even celebrate the day you were born because Jeremy is not here?" That is when I really realized that I had wrapped up most of my world in my husband. I mean, that is what we are supposed to do, right? We live our life as one when we are single, then when we become married, we live our life as the two becoming one. But what do you do when you drastically become just the one again? Could I celebrate life and experience new things even though he was no longer a part of it?

I can remember being so resistant to that in the early days. It makes you feel like by moving on that you are somehow dishonoring the life of your spouse or loved one. For example, I got the urge to repaint our bedroom several months after the accident. I got excited thinking about the color of the paint and even changed the bedding and curtains to be more feminine. Then the day came when it was all done and I stepped back to admire the room. The first thought that came to me was, "Jeremy would absolutely hate this room." I broke down and cried.

Now, I know that it was completely okay, and healthy even, to change the room, but I was not prepared for the emotional and mental attack. Another grief ambush. Initial grief and the firsts can be like that, so I share in order to tell you, friend, to be prepared to give yourself grace. It has taken you years to build the life that you had with your spouse or loved one, and now it is gone so quickly and you will need time to rebuild. I know that maybe, even as you read this, you might be thinking, "I do not have the energy to rebuild!" Or perhaps, "I do not want to rebuild because I loved what had been built before!"

Friend, I hear you and feel you. I felt and thought those exact same things, but here is what I know personally. You are not in any way dishonoring your loved one by moving forward. You are not moving on because in grief you cannot "move on" as you will always carry some of them with you. You are who you are because of the love and influence that person had on your life. Moving forward means you are carrying forward the parts and pieces of them that they gave to you as you learn to survive in this journey.

Change the paint. Move the furniture. Change holidays and special gatherings to what suits you and maybe honors them in a new way. Hold space with the grief and have conversations with others on what traditions could look like in the here and now. That first year of firsts, the kids and I did our best just to survive them. That is okay, too. The second year, we had good conversations about what things we wanted to keep and honor and what things and traditions we were okay with changing or even skipping.

There is no right or wrong way. This journey will be as unique as you and your family are, and there is beauty in that uniqueness. This, however, is what I would not recommend. I would not recommend changing nothing and keeping things exactly the same way they have always been. I also would not recommend trying to mask the pain through alcohol, drugs, sex, gambling, shopping, pornography, etc. Finally, do not shut everyone out of the process and isolate yourself. It is healthy to talk and process. Brave friend, be willing to make some changes on your time when you are ready. Believe me, I know this is awful and hard, I get that acutely. Again, there is beauty in the ashes if we are brave enough to look and see.

CHAPTER 9

Grief Speaks and then Comes Healing

"Yet I still dare to hope when I remember this: The faithful love of the Lord never ends! His mercies never cease. Great is his faithfulness; his mercies begin afresh each morning."
Lamentations 3:21-23 (NLT)

"DEAR SISTER, WILL you please let yourself heal!" I read the words of my wise mentor in Facebook Messenger like he had said something in Greek. I thought to myself, *What does he mean, let myself heal? I am not sick!* If he would have been standing in front of me, I probably would have given him a bewildered look. Instead of responding, I decided to chew on what he said first. As I went about my day, there was a moment when I was replaying his conversation over in my mind and the Holy Spirit whispered, "Your heart is sick."

Can you have a sick heart? Can your heart need healing? All of my theology and scripture references seemed null and void in the moment of revelation; my heart absolutely was sick and needed deep, deep healing. Grief inflicts such a hard pain, such a deep penetrating blow, that does not just affect your persona, but it also deeply affects your physical, mental, emotional, and spiritual core.

My husband gave me a gift one time that he and the kids had made. It was a heart made out of metal and welded together, of course, and inside he had a photocopied piece of paper with information he had found on the internet about the effects of the heart. I found it while cleaning out a closet after the accident. It was a gift that I had completely forgotten about. At one point, the article gives stats on the knowledge that you can die of a broken heart. Who would have ever thought you can actually die from a broken heart? I now have that heart, with that photocopied paper, sitting on the table where his ashes sit in our dining room. How, though, do you heal something internally that feels like it tried to stop beating the day your loved one passed?

If you are grieving, I am sure you have heard all of the horrible cliches that get spoken to those who are grieving, but nevertheless, they tell you that you should be grateful that you got to love someone so hard. Somehow, they think it will bring you comfort to remind you that you got to experience that kind of love once. Please do not ever say this to someone who is grieving. Ever. The truth is those kinds of statements never bring comfort. The only thing those phrases do is inflict more pain as, again, you are acutely reminded of what has been lost. If I had not loved my husband so deeply, my heart would not be broken. But to not love so deeply would be an absolute crime against God and humanity. We were created to love and be loved.

Could my broken heart heal, though, without the love and support of my husband? It is a complex thing, really. Your spouse, or maybe even a parent or close friend, who has passed, would be the perfect person to help heal your heart in this devastating situation. But the irony is, they are not here to help. And often, that makes the pain even worse.

Who is going to hold me while I sob tears that seem to come from the depths of my soul? Who is going to walk with me and give me sound advice on what needs to be done next? Who is going to make me laugh and forget for just a moment the shocking horror that they are gone? Whose chest can I lay my head on to speak my burdens and let my new guard down for just a moment?

Another phrase that very good and well-intentioned people will say is, "I pray you can feel the loving arms of God surround you." To be honest, I hated that phrase. Do you know why? I could not feel God's loving arms surrounding me, at least not in the beginning. Again, if I am honest, I would have preferred to have felt the warm, strong, flesh and blood arms of my husband.

I can remember in those beginning days of horror after the accident that my son was really struggling, naturally. I tried to console him, again with the words that I thought would bring comfort, that "at least" his dad was with God and we had the hope of seeing him again one day (by the way, never use the phrase "at least" with someone who is grieving).

We know that those of us who have hope in Christ know this is true, and my hurting and grieving son honestly responded, "I would rather have my dad back than to have Jesus." Feel the honesty of that for a minute. Friends, I can speak openly about this because I know it to be true. God was not afraid of my son's honesty in that moment, nor was God angry with him for trying to articulate the great pain of grief.

I never used that phrase on him again, and you know what? God was faithful to begin healing his broken heart, too. So often, God does not need us to say anything to comfort someone who is grieving. This is the biggest lesson I have learned from the Book of Job. The biggest mistake made by Job's friends is they grew tired of sitting with him in his grief and they thought, somehow, they could use words to try and help mend Job's heart. No, friends. Only God can mend a broken heart and only when you let Him. It would not be too long after this that my son would recommit his life and I had the treasure of watching him choose to be baptized. It stole my breath away to see the glorious smile on his face as he came out of the water, again a new creation.

So often people say "grief is a journey," and again, honestly, I have never cared for that phrase. One, because usually when I think of a journey, I think of a trip and trips tend to be fun. But perhaps I need to rethink what the word means in my mind. I am reminded of the two friends traveling on the road to Emmaus in scripture (Luke 24:13-36) after the crucifixion of Jesus. They were confused, perplexed, and very sorrowful, but they could not stay where they were, they had to travel. I am sure it was not a "fun" trip for them, except for one point. The point where Jesus shows up, and while they did not recognize Him, He traveled with them the rest of the way.

Grief is like that in so many ways. You cannot stay with a broken heart forever. You also cannot turn your back on and avoid grief because it is so painful. No, you have to take a step forward, however and whenever you are ready. It is going to be painful and it is going to be confusing. It is going to be full of sorrow and it may not have a foreseeable ending. But when you remember that Jesus walks with you, then you truly will never walk alone.

Even if it feels like everyone has abandoned you, I promise God has not. Even if it feels like no one around you can speak the language of grief, I promise you Jesus can. Even if it feels like you do not know which direction to go, the Holy Spirit is ready to guide you. The journey is hard and long, and you are going to want to quit, give up, and let that broken heart of yours give out and die. But even while I am still traversing down this broken, winding, pothole-filled road, too, I know that God will see each one of us through because He really is a good, good Father and you really are loved by Him.

Sending God's hope and peace to you, my friend, for your journey. Grief speaks… then comes healing.

Printed in the USA
CPSIA information can be obtained
at www.ICGtesting.com
CBHW070234120324
5226CB00018B/41